Singing from the First Eve

Lillith May

Presentation by *BookLeaf Publishing*

Web: www.bookleafpub.com

E-mail: info@bookleafpub.com

ISBN: 9789357441094

First edition 2023

DEDICATION

For T, my cat.

Break Champagne Against This Vessel

I christen the start with resolutions;
The Captain's quite convinced
To strive toward - 'fore this journeys end -
Worthy accomplishments -

And here, behold - my losses and wins,
A bounty found in effort;
Gold in triumph, something learned in trying,
All shining - hoarded Treasure

Even shipwrecks inspire ballads that move,
So sailor - I enquire again:
  In what ways - could this faring improve,
  And prove - my time well-spent?

The Apples in Fables

2

Our Libraries still stand as forests;
How proud the mighty book!
Fine fruits found from the harvest,
Wilde pages - like living wood -

And to taste one! I'll swallow the seeds -
By slight pip, secret stone,
Or samarae falling on me as I read;
Tended there, they'll Grow -

Oh, I've seen orchards richer than Queens -
Behind the eyes of the curious;
They follow paths lined with trees - wherever they lead
And return with jeweled branches on their words

Poe's Ponderment

3

Were I to kiss - the Lute of Olde -
Found - in antiquity,
The notes would fly - in rosen gold;
For Lips - Free Currency

Yet if Yesterday - filtered every tune,
Left fresher lyrics - scarce,
Slanted relevance - would halt my bloom,
And Tomorrow - would forget.

Modus Operandi

I trade my blade - for gentle flowers,
My spiders - for fine silk,
Then kiss the rose, bleed the hour -
By my love's thorns to bilk

And I, the villain, wrote my Truth;
Still close - to a sin,
I split the word - by gossamer tooth -
To let the fabric sing

You adore the beauty more my dear,
So I'll try to spin it well,
Weaving melancholies - to wily briars -
And tears - to sweeter petals -

Faux Fleur

Plastic stems, petals in pastel tulle;
Immortality when I was never alive.
I'd hate to be - a pretending thing,
With a grace that never fades -
And a Grace - that sweetly lies.

Some Questions for my Mortality

Does Death long greatly to greet me,
Eager to Meet - one day? -
Or does he take me - regretfully,
Sorry - I couldn't stay -

And does dear Life like to have me,
Do I offer her - Any grace?
Or will she be glad - once I'm away,
Bound - for some other Place!

For Tomb and Tome

They said their words then stood as Stone;
Seasons become a day -
When Time unveils the Passing
Before a Perfect face

Some souls content with silence -
Might hope sing Eterne,
Once quelled voices - locked in Earth -
Rise upon the Dawn

Yet my Immortals command I listen -
To old and extant echoes:
There's a breath to patina complexions,
Epitaphs - where moss Grows -

Gilded Graves

But mourn not those in marble mausoleums;
In vainglory of Steep tombs -
And monuments - are the cold testaments -
To what rich ghosts can afford

For even though death has moved them,
Their homes still survive ours;
Empty pockets - made discount coffins -
Where Existence is charged

Tis cheaper to burn! The poor masses to ashes,
And our evidence - to dust.
There's a fee to die, and a fee to Live,
And no way - to flee the Cost.

Classes in Operating Theatres

This is The Country - a mortal body:
Cells made civilians,
Organs composed from diverse cities,
A gorvernment - as brain

Distribution of life's blood Divided,
A few deprived of oxygen;
Entire limbs will starve and die -
If prioritising wins -

"I'm as healthy as my most functioning part!"
Said the island to the doctor,
"Though if you're treating - free of charge -
  I might need some looking after -"

The Student

What is not for me to Know -
I seek - more fervently,
Rarely do I find before -
Why - 't was kept from me

And if the Sun - shines too bright -
Whilst educating - Day,
Why then - I stare - 'til I'm blind,
And I find Night - another way -

Texture

Oh - all the muslin, tulle, silk, and satin!
No fabric could compare -
To the great graces of your saintly skin,
Sun-blessed, and bare -

And I wonder if she who fixed the mind -
Tailored the Tyger, too;
Divinity sewn - where fierce beasts strike,
Kisses stitched - where they maul -

And I'm cold, lend me your soul to wear;
I'll worship - how you Feel,
Then send a prayer - to that stylish creature,
For Love - or for a Kill -

Delicate Days

In the fragile Chambers - of my little World -
I feel - an abject thunder,
It bellows in turmoil - about the timid Soul,
And Tears all hope asunder.

It seems so precarious, to me - to Exist,
To be Certain, I'm unsure;
I'm the beacon of Light! - for all of a minute,
Then rain, and I'm - No More -

Crooked Smiles and Feathers

13

I cherish my Joy, that meek birdling:
Downy - golden yellow,
Fragile - with one broken wing;
I hold it - in my soul

When I'm well, that small thing -
Feels well too!
And it flies slant - and it sings,
Every morn - to woo

And with all the giggles and grins -
My faerie grew;
I hope for it to forget its affliction,
To find its wind -
    and Fly True -

My Apathy as Franc
(a fat cat)

Here - Muse, his Cheshire grin's now fading;
See, behind his white whiskers -
There's rows of fine teeth faintly gleaming
Through smiles of absent care

And heavy paws - rich in fur - tread surfaces,
Making sure that I'm aware -
My laptop, paper, books - are his resting places;
Work halts when he's near

He obstructs my routines with outright remiss -
In an effortless sort of way,
As though that beast need only exist -
To disrupt my day

And Oh! My dear pen is just a toy to him,
When he even bothers play;
Ah! But if I use it for anything else, then -
He vanishes:

        head…

           tail…

              …

Ribbit

I must have left the back door open
In one of my dreams last night,
Because I woke up this morning
With a frog in my lungs, and -
A pond - in my brain.

Around noon -
It went for a swim behind my eyes,
And collected all the scum
That had begun to gather there
Into a rusty bucket.

Two hours later,
It sat on my tongue, and -
Wrote its name on the backs of my teeth
With a stick of old charcoal,
Before it waved goodbye -

Leapt onto the page,

And -

Got my paper all wet.

Influence or Influenza

Bless me, for curse of that first forsaken contact!
A fierce virus met my palm;
Scarcely a soul immune - to the Touch that infects,
Be it by germ - or catching charm

Came down with it quickly, I've been sick ever since,
Affected by all manner of malady;
I noted my symptoms, had prescriptions written,
Even found a word for my disease -

I'm weak, but still following remedies to the letter -
And hoping - the fever breaks;
Come tomorrow - will I know I'm getting better?
Or will I only find - it's killed Me?

Read This With Your Mask On:

I feel I might myself be the disease,
The despairing illness, the vile virus,
And I'm pretty sure I'm catching -
                              so don't Touch!
Lest you find yourself infected;

Then - how dire, there'll be a pair of us;
A verbal pandemic! Some sickly poets -
Spewing words in place of bile, and -
Using paper scraps
                              to catch our coughs.

Mona Lisa has a Whisper -

Artists - often too timid to offer a word,
Yet still brave enough to Touch;
Tracing the corners - of verklempt worlds -
With quills - dipped in Blush

These light brushstrokes seem a mild affair,
'Til parchment trembles in reply -
To mute earthquakes - and queer wildfires -
There painted - by the Shy

Should even the softest utterance fly free,
Fierce silences would be broken;
To think - if just their palms have wrecked me,
What then - when They have Spoken?

There's a hesitance before the Gallery

I'm not as brave as the peacocks -
No advertisements - here;
My colours kept - like slight secrets -
Cautious - to ever Share

And when I do - dare Participate,
As Naked as winter's tree,
My plumage on that far display -
Leaves nought - for modesty

Yet colder - still, when to Night
Feathers get locked away;
Scarcely seen, long out of sight,
And missing - the light of Day.

The Floral Dialect

You plant words like wanton flowers -
Of crimson silk, and plush;
Tended hearts - or gardens - still overgrown,
Blooming - to Wilde blush

Your beguiling briars - guard the Treasures -
By covert hedge - and bush,
Dressing sylvan minds in ivy undertones -
And hints - of scarlet lush

Faye, never hush your pastoral verses,
And hate to prune the gush,
For your thickets - your true June Roses -
Have new grovers - Touched -

I seek a Treasure -

Oh - I never found myself in a Day,
A Year neither;
I've found her in pieces!

In the fire of my bliss -
In velvet kissed -
In opportunities missed,
In things I didn't say;
I've found her in October,
In the Winter Weather,
And in May;

I can find her only when she's been lost,
Only after -
I've given Her away -